Prologue

THE Ring gleamed. Its gold circle seemed to smile as it lay under the water. The current lifted it slightly, and then dropped it. It seemed to be waiting, coiling round and round like the great serpent of Middle Earth that swallows its own tail. As it shifted in the water it seemed to wink its one eye, as if it knew . . .

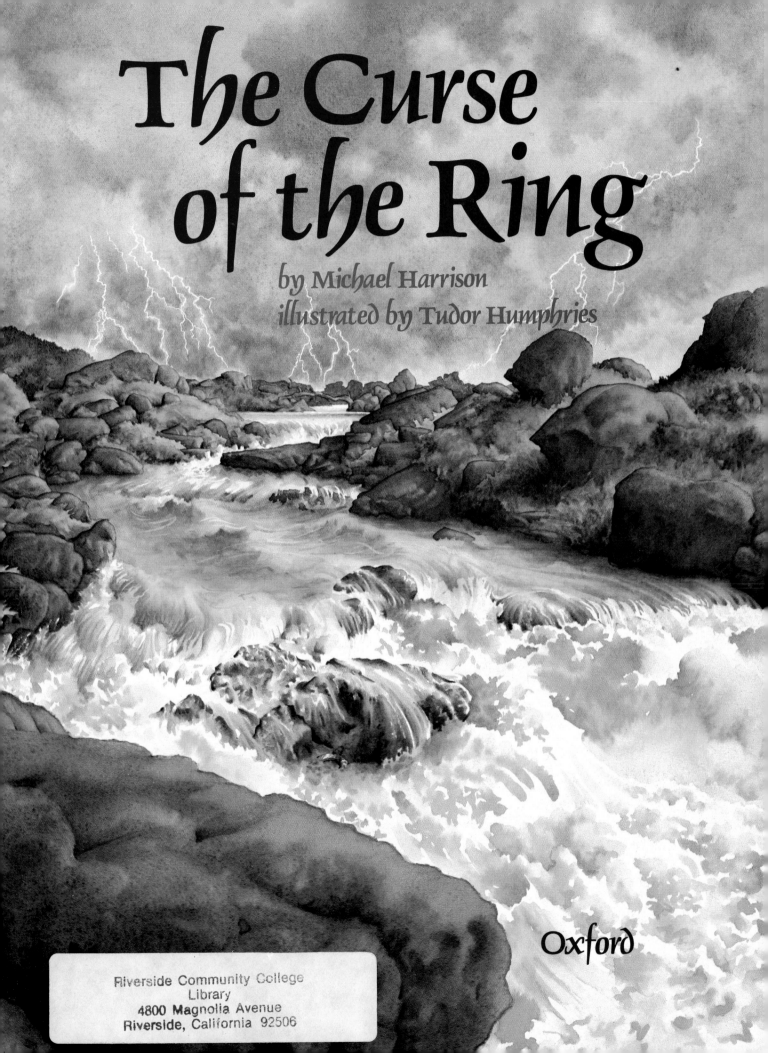

The Curse of the Ring

by Michael Harrison
illustrated by Tudor Humphries

Oxford

Oxford University Press, Walton Street, Oxford OX2 6DP

Oxford New York Toronto
Delhi Bombay Calcutta Madras Karachi
Petaling Jaya Singapore Hong Kong Tokyo
Nairobi Dar es Salaam Cape Town
Melbourne Auckland

and associated companies in
Beirut Berlin Ibadan Nicosia

Oxford is a trade mark of Oxford University Press

Text © Michael Harrison 1987

Illustrations © Tudor Humphries 1987

First published 1987

ISBN 0 19 274131 4

British Library Cataloguing in Publication Data
Harrison, Michael, *1939—*
The curse of the ring.
I. Title II. Humphries, Tudor

ISBN 0-19-274131-4

Phototypeset by Tradespools Limited, Frome, Somerset
Printed in Hong Kong

How the Ring Came into the World of Men

IT was Loki who started it, of course. Loki wasn't quite a god, though he lived in Asgard, the land of the gods, and was a friend of the gods. Trouble followed Loki around like his shadow. If he didn't start trouble, he was there when it happened.

This story begins when Loki was on a journey through Middle Earth with two of the gods, Honir and Odin. They were disguised, as always. Odin, the father of the gods, wore a faded blue cloak and a broad-brimmed hat pulled down at the front to shade his missing eye. Loki was dressed as a poor farmer with a woollen cap covering his flaming red hair. Honir had less need of disguise and eyes passed over him incuriously.

They had been walking through birchwoods deep in talk, paying no attention to where they were going. They had been speaking of the Norns, the three women who sit under one of the roots of the great Ash Tree. The Norns spend their day weaving on a giant loom. What they weave is fate, the fate of men and of gods. Their hooded heads are bent over the pattern, weaving in one thread,

6

cutting off another. As they weave, so events fall out.

Was the conversation of the three gods part of the pattern, so that they lost their way? Or had the concentration of their minds attracted the Norns and caused them to add the gods into their work? However it was, they found themselves on the bank of a stream that splashed noisily over stones. The sun was going down and long beams of light shone through the trees and glinted like gold on the water.

'Where do we go now?' asked Honir.

'You'd better ask Loki,' said Odin. 'He travels round Middle Earth more than I do. He should be able to find us a lodging for the night.'

'Well, Loki?' began Honir, but Loki held up his hand for silence. Then he bent down, picked up a stone from the bank of the stream, and flung it hard. The other two leant forward to see what he had thrown at but Loki plunged into the stream. He waded through to the opposite bank and then turned. He held in his hands a dead otter, with a salmon in its mouth.

'How's that for one shot?' he shouted. 'Food and clothing at once – or payment for a night's shelter. And look, there is smoke between the trees.'

The other two splashed across the stream to join him. As they pulled themselves up the bank Loki explained how he had seen the otter lying with the fish it had caught.

'Two with one stone,' he said.

They walked cheerfully towards the plume of smoke they could see through the trees, not thinking any more about the Norns and fate. As they drew nearer they saw a stoutly-built farmhouse in a clearing.

Down the hillside, on either side of the stream, were fields of ripe barley. The place looked prosperous and secure.

As they approached, the farmer came out. Odin spoke first.

'Greetings! We are travellers who have lost our way. We need lodgings for the night, and supper.'

Hreidmar, the farmer, looked at them. He saw three men: two peasants, one . . . not a farmer by his clothes or his voice, more like a magician. Hreidmar himself was a powerful black magician, as well as a strong farmer. He wanted no competitor, and no spying on him by another of his craft.

'We have no room,' he said.

Loki pushed forward now, still delighted with his throw. 'We can pay,' he said, 'even though hospitality demands that you feed us for nothing.' And he held out the bodies of the salmon and the otter.

Hreidmar looked coldly at Loki's hands, and then at his face. He turned and led them into the house.

'Sit,' he said, pointing to stools by the fire. He went out again and called. Two figures came through the doorway behind him. One was a tall, sullen-looking, young man. The other was a short, stocky-looking boy.

'Now my three sons are present,' he said, 'you should introduce yourselves.'

Odin looked round. 'Three?'

'This is Fafnir,' Hreidmar said, pointing to the young man. 'And this is Regin,' pointing to the boy.

'Yes, yes,' said Odin, scarcely polite. 'But where is the third son? Is he so small that we can't see him?'

'Your friend is holding him,' said Hreidmar, pointing at Loki. 'See my son, my dead son, Otter.'

Loki came forward slowly and placed the otter and the salmon on the table.

'I threw the stone that killed him,' he said. 'But how can he be your son?'

'My son is, was, a Shape-Changer. He loved to play in the water as a child. He loved the streamlined shape of an otter and used to swim for hours in the stream. Now you have killed him with an idle throw. You will pay with your red blood.'

9

The gods saw now they were trapped. Hreidmar stood with his back to the door, an axe in his right hand. Fafnir and Regin had come in from harvesting the fields of barley. They had scythes in their hands. The gods had no weapons and could not use their powers because they were in human form. Loki's quick tongue was all they had and, as so often, that was enough.

'Why kill us, when we can offer you blood-money for your son? Gold ringing down on this very table.'

'Gold!' said Hreidmar. 'Where would the likes of you get enough gold to pay the blood-price for my son? I will have the satisfaction of cleaving you into joints of raw meat now.'

As he raised his axe Loki began to speak. He spoke of gold until they could almost see it gleaming in the shadowy room, until the yearning for the yellow metal leaped up in Hreidmar's heart and swamped his sorrow for his son. He lowered his axe and said:

'I will give you twenty-four hours. If you return with enough gold to fill the otter skin so that it stands upright and then to cover it so that not a hair shows, then you may all go. If not, then I will have my price in blood. And you two,' he pointed his axe at Odin and Honir, 'will act as my hostages. You,' and here he came close and leant the keen iron blade on Loki's chest, 'you will fetch the gold.'

Loki smiled at Hreidmar, at Fafnir, at Regin. He lifted one hand in salute to Odin and Honir, and was gone. Hreidmar pushed some slices of barley bread across the table and poured out mugs of ale.

'Feast,' he said mockingly, 'while you can.'

They all sat down, and waited.

As Loki came out of the farmhouse the smile left his face. The dwarfs who lived and mined underground had plenty of gold but it would take days to find them in their maze of tunnels. He only had hours. Where could he find gold quickly, and enough to fill and cover the otter skin? Loki brooded on the dwarfs. They had been made from maggots that had bred in the body of Ymir the father of the giants. They lived underground as miners and smiths. Then he smiled again. He had remembered Andvari. Andvari was a dwarf, but he did not live under the earth like the other dwarfs. One story was that he had been caught thieving and had been banished. Another story said that he had amassed so much gold that he was afraid of its being stolen and so he had crept away from the mines and forges to . . .

Loki followed the bank of the stream as it splashed its way down through the forest. (Did the Norns smile as they saw Loki walking towards Andvari, or were they too busy weaving the future?) When Andvari had left the underground tunnels of the dwarfs he had come to live in a cave underneath a waterfall. And that waterfall was on this very stream. It was strange, thought Loki, how Shape-Changing kept recurring. He was a Shape-Changer himself, Otter had been, and Andvari was too. Andvari the Dwarf spent much of his time as a salmon. Here Loki stopped abruptly, and groaned aloud. Otter had

11

held in his mouth a large, dead salmon. Then he laughed. If the dead salmon was Andvari, why then the gold was lying ready for the first taker. And if the salmon was not, then he would have to use his wits to get it.

So Loki walked downstream. The full moon rose and lit his path, the white light falling through the birch leaves and shining off the trunks. He ate late strawberries that he found along the bank and chewed grains of barley he had picked in Hreidmar's field. Towards dawn he heard the sound of the waterfall. The first light was shining on the spray, making a miniature rainbow bridge across the water as he reached the top of the fall. Loki sat quietly on the edge and looked down, letting his eyes follow the falling water into the depths of the pool below. He saw a large salmon hovering in the broken water. He sat and thought. A picture came into his mind: a salmon, in the mouth of . . .

It was so quick. First Loki, sitting quietly at the top of the waterfall, his red hair catching the morning sun, the sliding green water, the salmon in the eddying pool. Then Loki dived into the water and an otter surfaced. The otter swam back to the bank, a fine salmon held firmly in its mouth. The fish gasped in the air like a drowning man, flapped and . . . there was the dwarf held firmly in Loki's hands.

'What do you want with me?' growled Andvari.

Loki smiled. 'Just your gold.'

'Gold? What gold would I have here?'

Loki gently tightened his fingers on Andvari's neck.

'I am Loki, friend of Odin, dweller in Asgard. I am Loki, Shape-Changer. What shall I turn myself into to give you the most painful, the most long-drawn-out death – before I take your gold for myself? A snake that will squeeze you hour by hour, squeeze the breath from your body, squeeze the ribs until they collapse inwards and pierce your heart? A ravening lion to eat you from your toes upwards, joint by joint?' Loki's fingers tightened little by little to increase the pressure that his words were applying to Andvari. Then the dwarf could take no more and he put his hands together in a sign of submission.

'I will give you all the gold you need,' Andvari gasped as soon as he could speak again.

'I thought you might see sense,' said Loki. Andvari led him to his

12

cave behind the waterfall. Here in the dim light that came through the roaring water, gold gleamed. Loki picked up some rabbit skins from the floor and knotted the legs together to make a bag. He thrust the gold into it. When all was in he looked carefully round the cave in case there was more gold hidden. He turned over skins and bones with one foot, running his hand through the straw that was Andvari's bed. Satisfied, he turned to go. Then he stopped, and grasped the dwarf by the wrist. He smiled as he drew out from under Andvari's sleeve, over Andvari's hand, an arm-ring of twisting snakes eating each others' tails.

At this the dwarf, who had stood in sullen silence till now, let out a cry of misery: 'Not this! Leave me this ring and I can use it to make more gold. Take it from me and I have naught.'

Loki laughed cruelly. 'I need all this gold. But I will name this ring after you. I shall call it Andvaranaut, for indeed Andvari has naught left.'

Then Andvari raised his voice and said:

'I curse this Ring
And he who will own it.
Let the darkness of the rock from which it was dug
Crush him.
Let the heat of the furnace in which it was refined
Burn him.
Let the blows of the hammer with which it was forged
Break him.
Let confusion ring him round.
Let emptiness fill his heart.'

Loki stood smiling. Andvari believed that Loki wanted the gold for himself. But Loki had no intention of keeping the gold. It, and the curse, would go to Hreidmar. So the dwarf did not curse Loki because he could not believe that anyone could give the gold away.

Loki was still smiling when he walked into Hreidmar's farmhouse and emptied the rabbit-skin bag on the table. Odin's hand was suddenly lying on top of the Ring, Andvaranaut. Loki shook his head at him but Odin turned his one eye away for even he felt the pull of the gold.

Fafnir quickly skinned the dead Otter and pushed the smallest bits of gold inside until the fur bulged and stood upright. Then Hreidmar stepped forward and heaped the larger gold pieces over the gold-stuffed Otter until the whole animal was covered, and all the gold was gone.

'There,' said Odin, 'our blood-debt is paid in full. Now let us go.'

But Hreidmar hoped for both blood and gold and hastily scanned the heap until he gave a cry of triumph:

'Here is one whisker uncovered! You have not fulfilled your side of the bargain and,' here he reached behind him for his axe, 'you must die.'

Odin raised his hand slowly. There on the table lay the Ring. 'This is enough to cover one whisker,' he said, and got to his feet to go. Hreidmar ignored the gods as they left. He was too busy turning the Ring between his fingers.

'Goodbye,' said Loki, as he left the farmhouse, 'and may all Andvari's wishes be granted.' And so he passed from the story, and returned with Honir and Odin from Middle Earth to Asgard, his part finished.

'Now, Father,' said Fafnir, 'let us share the gold between us. You have lost a son, but we have lost a brother.'

Hreidmar shook his head. He pulled a wooden chest towards the table and started to fill it with the gold. Still he said nothing, but seemed to sing as one might over a new baby in a cradle. Fafnir touched Regin on the arm and led him outside.

'It is not right that that old man should have all that,' he burst out. 'What does he need gold for at his age? We need it more, for we have our lives before us.'

His young brother nodded. He had been dazzled by the treasure but had not expected to share in it; little came his way but blows and work. Now he was being offered more than he could ever have dreamed of.

'But what can we do?'

Fafnir smiled. He went back into the farmhouse, picked up the axe, and swept Hreidmar's head from his shoulders as he was bending over the table. The red blood poured over the gold. Regin shrank back. He

was young, and this was his first death. Fafnir put his hand on the Ring,
turned, and saw him cringing in the shadows. He raised his axe, the
blood dripping in the red firelight.

'Keep away, this is mine now,' Fafnir snarled. He flung down the
axe. He crammed the gold back into the rabbit-skin bag and carried it
out of the farmhouse. Regin at first stood, slumped against the wall, but
then he thought:

My brothers gone, my father dead on the floor, the axe that killed him here. I will be accused of the killings. And so Regin followed Fafnir as his brother lurched under the weight of the gold in the moonlight. He saw him go into a cave in the hillside above the forest. He crept closer and heard Fafnir taking the gold out of his sack, crooning over each piece. Shocked and tired, Regin fell asleep.

In the morning he went to the cave and called out, 'Fafnir!'

His brother came to the mouth of the cave and snarled at him, 'Go away! This is mine now and I will guard it with my life.'

Regin stared at his brother. Fafnir seemed changed, monstrous. His foul breath sickened Regin and Fafnir's rage seemed to burn him up. He turned and ran, ran from the cave, from Fafnir, from the gold. He would return.

The Dragon and the Sword

IT was some weeks before Regin came back to the cave. All the time the tapestry of the Norns grew longer. Under their silent hands patterns were repeated and lives were doomed.

This time Regin approached cautiously. He hid behind a thicket of gorse. Here he sat and waited in the cold early morning. The land seemed stiller and bleaker than he remembered. Strange noises came from the cave, making him alert and nervous. Then, from out of the mouth of the cave came a dragon, scaly, grey, evil. Its small red eyes flicked short-sightedly from side to side. The beast slowly crawled down the hill to the stream at the bottom. Quickly Regin ran to the mouth of the cave.

'Fafnir! Fafnir!' he called, but there was no answer. As the rays of the rising sun shone into the darkness within, he saw the gold spread out, as straw might be spread out for cows. There was no sign of his brother.

'Fafnir!' he shouted in despair, and saw to his horror the dragon raise its head from the water and turn towards him. The dreadful truth came to him: *that* was his brother. With a cry that he gulped back in terror he ran stumbling and gasping away.

Regin wandered northwards. He stopped for a while in a village and helped the old smith in exchange for shelter. Here he discovered in himself a talent for the work. But he could not settle, and so he wandered on through the years.

All the time he brooded on revenge, and on the gold. He knew he was not brave enough to fight the dragon himself. What he needed was

one of the great heroes of the past, a dragon-slayer. Then, as he travelled from village to village, he heard of a hero called Sigmund, and of his marvellous sword.

Each village had a slightly different story to tell, and Regin listened eagerly to them all. They all agreed that Sigmund was a mighty warrior and that he had received his sword directly from Odin. In one village he was told of a great marriage feast for a king's daughter. When all had drunk well an old man had walked in, an old man in a faded blue cloak and a wide-brimmed hat. He had walked up to the great tree the hall had been built round and plunged a sword straight into the trunk of the tree, right up to its hilt. Of course, everyone had tried to pull it out, but no one succeeded until Sigmund had laid his hand on it and then it had slid out as easy as easy.

Regin always asked where Sigmund could be found, and always received an answer that was half-different. Every time he was told of a place where Sigmund had been—and was then told, 'Or he might be with his friend, King Vendel.' So it was not surprising that time and miles brought Regin to the court of King Vendel. Vendel was a just and kind man, and the Norns wove his kindness into their design.

Regin came to his Hall and asked for work. It was the beginning of harvest and so there was more than enough for an extra smith. The stranger proved himself a good workman and so was made welcome. Regin worked hard but said little, and nothing about his past.

Vendel's son, Ilf, had been out voyaging for the summer months and his return was eagerly awaited day by day. His men would return with goods they had bartered for and, more important, with stories for the dark winter evenings.

At last the sails and dragon-prows were seen approaching the harbour. Regin left his forge, as he always did when ships were sighted. Perhaps this time there would be news of the hero Sigmund. He joined the people crowding the quay to watch the ships come in. As Ilf's ship drew nearer they could see two young women sitting in the back, near the helmsman, well wrapped against the wind. A murmur of surprise ran round. Although it was common enough to buy slaves, or capture women from a defeated enemy, Ilf had always been too noble a man to drag anyone away from their home, or to allow his men to do so. Had he changed? The oars were shipped, the mooring ropes thrown up and made fast, the ladder let down. The watchers saw Ilf helping the women as if they were honoured guests. They climbed up on to the quay. King Vendel stepped forward and clasped his son. Ilf spoke quietly, and then the King led the two women away towards his Hall. As the crowd parted to let them through they saw the women's faces—one dark-haired, dressed as a queen; one fair, as a servant. The dark one—smiling nervously, eyes down; the fair one—looking straight ahead, tears sliding down cheeks. Then the strangers were forgotten in the happiness of seeing loved ones again. Regin had no loved ones. He

watched, little knowing what had landed.

After dinner in Vendel's Hall Ilf started the story of his journeyings. He began in the middle, at the part that concerned the two women. As he spoke, in the flickering light of fire and torches, his hearers saw in their minds the picture his words created. They saw the ships sailing up the Great River in the evening sun.

'To our surprise,' Ilf said, 'we saw a small group of ships launched hastily from a shelving beach and saw them rowed away round a sweeping bend until they were hidden by trees. We ran out our oars and rowed to the beach. Standing in the bows, and shading my eyes, I saw, silhouetted against the setting sun, two women clasped together. I jumped down into the shallow water and started to run towards them. As I pulled myself up the bank of the river I stopped suddenly. There, on the grass, there had been a battle, and many killed. I walked slowly across the blood-stained grass, looking, listening for the wounded, but there were none.'

There was silence in the Hall as they listened to Ilf's story. Regin, standing in the shadows beyond the firelight, leant forwards as Ilf continued.

'The women were Queen Hiordis and her maid. At their feet lay
Sigmund, dead.'

A groan came from every mouth in Vendel's Hall, every mouth
except Regin's. He was shocked into silence as his dreams and plans
were shattered at that moment.

'Sigmund? Dead?' cried King Vendel.

'Sigmund lying dead,' replied Ilf, 'and his great sword, Cleave, in
two pieces beside him.'

'Lord Vendel,' the beautiful servant woman said stepping forward,
'the only reason Sigmund was killed was that Odin wanted him for
Valhalla. If he had died of old age he would have gone to Hel. A
Valkyrie shattered his sword—and they only act at Odin's command.'

Regin looked at the two women and noticed as the servant stood
forwards that she looked as if she would have a child before many
months had passed. Ideas began to swirl in his head like the smoke that
twisted up from the fire.

'Go on with your story, my son,' said Vendel, tears beginning to run
down his cheeks.

So Ilf spoke again of the scene on the river bank; the two women

silhouetted against the blood-stained sky, and lying on the grass, with the dying sun casting long grotesque shadows, men in the contorted attitudes of violent death. Ilf had told the women that they had nothing to fear from him, and promised to take them to their home. At this they had grown agitated. They explained that Sigmund had been killed by the evil King Lyngvi because he had wanted Queen Hiordis for himself. If they returned home Lyngvi would pursue them.

So Ilf had ordered his men to prepare the dead for their journey to Valhalla and then had led the women down to the boats.

There was silence in Vendel's Hall as Ilf stopped speaking. Then the King broke it.

'You have been guided by the gods, my son. My friend Sigmund's queen is truly welcome in my Hall.'

As Vendel spoke kindly to the queen, Ilf looked again at the two women. He wondered why so much blood should be shed for this queen while such a maid stood by. Who could fail to love the maid?

As the weeks passed Ilf was often in the company of the servant woman. Vendel became concerned and spoke to his son.

'I know you are an honourable man, and would not harm a fugitive

26

to our court. I know too that you have too much sense to make an unsuitable marriage. Is it good for the woman, or for you, that you spend so much time in a servant's company? You would do better to woo Queen Hiordis.'

'Father, I cannot,' said Ilf. 'And I cannot see how such a servant can serve such a queen.'

King Vendel smiled to himself. Next time he sat next to the queen he said to her, 'My Lady, may I ask you a question? How is it that you are always awake so early in the morning? I often see you walking in the fields soon after dawn.'

'As a child I had to get up at dawn to milk my father's cows,' she replied, 'and the habit has never left me.'

Vendel smiled again, and talked of the autumn fruits along the hedgerows. Later he looked for the servant woman. He found her sitting by the fire, a spindle idle in her lap, her eyes on the flames.

'It is a strange country you are from,' Vendel said. The woman turned her face towards him in surprise. 'Do you not think it strange,' he went on, 'that a princess should rise at dawn each day to milk cows, and should know where the best blackberries are to be found. And is it not strange that a queen should have a servant, unmarried but plainly soon to have a baby?' And he laid his hand gently on her arm and smiled kindly at her.

Tears flowed again down the woman's cheeks. 'You are right,' she said. 'I am Queen Hiordis. My servant persuaded me to take her place when we were waiting for Ilf's fleet to land. We had hidden from Lyngvi and feared some new danger. With each day it became more difficult to tell you we had deceived you, especially when . . .'

'Especially when Ilf became attentive,' said the King.

'I feared I would not be believed,' said Hiordis. Vendel left her looking into the fire and went to find Ilf.

In the months that followed Hiordis married Ilf, and had a baby son. She named him Sigurd in memory of his dead father, Sigmund. The months turned to years. The contentment of daily life filled all their hearts, or so it seemed.

Even Regin was filled with new hope. The son of mighty Sigmund must be a great hero, a dragon-slayer, surely?

The Mending of the Sword

As soon as Sigurd could run about he would run to Regin's forge. Hiordis thought he loved seeing the hard iron glow red and bend and twist, the fire leap up when he worked the bellows for Regin, and the sparks fill the forge when the iron was hammered. She thought it was strange that Regin, who was always abrupt and surly with everyone else, should have time for the boy. He would welcome him with a quick smile, ask him to pump the bellows, talk to him man to man. So Regin became, perhaps, more like Sigurd's father than his step-father Ilf had time to be. Regin planned to use Sigurd to slay Fafnir but he found he had come to love him like the son he had never had.

It was natural, then, that Sigurd should take the broken sword he found to Regin. He held it out, tarnished, in two pieces, lying on the piece of torn cloth in which it had been wrapped. Regin looked in the boy's face and read there that Sigurd had found it in his mother's things, without her knowledge.

'That's a fine sword, now,' he said. He picked up the two pieces and fitted them together. He rubbed his finger over the runes engraved on the blade.

'My name is Cleave,' he read out loud.

'That was my father's sword,' said the boy. 'Sigmund's I mean, not Ilf's. My mother has told me the story of how his sword shattered as he fought face to face with the horrid Lyngvi. That was the only reason he was killed. Odin wanted him for Valhalla, Mother says, and so made his sword break. Will you mend it for her?'

Regin wrapped the sword carefully in the cloth. 'I will mend it when the time comes,' he said.

'What time?'

'We will know, you and I,' said Regin, giving the boy a smile which showed that the two of them shared a secret. 'Now, put it back carefully, and say nothing. And hurry back, I need your strong arms for pumping.'

From that time on Regin told Sigurd stories when they rested from the forge. He filled the boy's mind and heart with the deeds of great heroes, wielders of famous swords, slayers of dragons, avengers of dishonour.

As Sigurd grew older he was able to spend less time at the forge but he still slipped away from his schooling and his duties when he could. The friendship that had grown up between Sigurd and Regin remained strong through the years until his early manhood.

Regin's manner towards Sigurd changed, slowly, subtly. The ideas that had swirled in his head had left black stains, like soot on the roof-beams, and his love for the boy was twisted by the plans he had to get Fafnir's gold. He began to make Sigurd long for glory. He began to hint that Ilf, now King since Vendel had died, did not treat Sigurd like one of his own sons.

'And which of your step-father's horses did you ride today?' Regin would ask. 'It's strange he's not given you one of your own.' The truth was that Sigurd had no horse of his own because Ilf shared everything with him and he could take whatever horse he liked. Regin's remarks pricked the insecurity of his age so that he felt unwanted, unvalued, unloved.

'Father, may I have a horse of my own?' he asked abruptly one evening. Ilf turned and looked at him sadly.

'You may have which ever you like,' he replied.

'No, not one of yours. I mean one I can make my own, an unbroken colt that I will ride, and I alone.'

'Of course,' said Ilf. 'Go to the pasture tomorrow and choose whichever you would like.' Sigurd left the Hall with a word of thanks and Ilf with a heavier heart.

Sigurd was out early in the morning. He went, casually, into Regin's forge.

'Have you a halter I could use?' he asked. 'Ilf feels I should choose a horse of my own.'

Regin watched him go and smiled to himself. Sigurd walked down to the meadows by the river. Here the herd of horses ran, some broken in, some half-wild. Sigurd sat on a boulder at the edge of the field and looked at them all.

'How do I know which is best?' he said to himself, thinking he was alone.

'Drive them all through the river,' came a voice from behind him. Sigurd looked round quickly. An old man in a blue cloak, wearing a wide-brimmed hat that shaded his one missing eye, stood smiling at him. As Sigurd stood looking at him he became impatient. 'Drive them down, boy. Drive them across the river, and then you will know which to choose.'

Sigurd pulled a branch from the hedge and ran down the slope towards the horses, shouting and waving. He chased them into a corner of the field between hedge and river. He forced them into the icy water that flowed swiftly down from the mountains. By midstream they were forced to swim, and swim hard, but they all reached the far bank, climbed out, shook themselves, and began to graze. The slope was steeper on that side and the grass was thinner. One horse, as white as the rippling water, raised his head, snorted, and crossed back over the river. When he reached the meadow he began to graze again.

'That's the one for you,' came the voice again. 'He is of Sleipnir's blood. Put your halter on him.'

Sigurd walked gently up to the horse, speaking softly. He slipped the halter on him, and then pulled himself on to his back. The horse turned his head, whinnied, and stood patiently. Sigurd looked

triumphantly to where the old man had been, but he had gone. His voice seemed to come into Sigurd's ear, 'His name is Swift.'

When Sigurd told Regin what had happened he put down his hammer and said, 'That was Odin. Your father, Sigmund, was a favourite of his, and you are too, obviously. Sleipnir is his horse, the eight-legged foal Loki produced. The gods know what is due to you.'

Regin continued to build up Sigurd's discontent, suggesting that he should have gold of his own to spend. When he seemed to have hooked him with the greed of gold he played him like a fish by talking again of great heroes, and of dragon-killers.

'Honour must come first,' said Sigurd. 'My father's death has not been avenged. The wicked Lyngvi still lives.'

'Come, now,' said Regin, almost sneering, 'what revenge is it if a penniless nobody kills him? He might as well be killed by a thief, or by accident. For revenge to be perfect you must kill him when you are so rich and so famous that everyone will know that you did it for honour – and not for gain or glory.'

'That sounds noble indeed,' said Sigurd, 'but it could take years to win to that position, and old age might claim Lyngvi first.'

31

Regin saw that Sigurd was now within his power and he talked to him for the first time of Fafnir on his hoard of gold. He spoke of the glory and riches that might be won with one blow of his sword. 'And then, Lyngvi,' he said.

Sigurd's heart flamed up but his mind was cautious. He questioned Regin carefully about the dragon.

'No ordinary sword will do. I would not have more than one chance. It must be strong and sharp.'

Regin went over to his bench and came back with a new sword.

'This I made today,' he said.

Sigurd grasped the sword in both hands, swung it over his head, and brought it clashing down on the anvil that stood between them. Regin leapt back as sparks and pieces of sword shot through the forge. Sigurd laughed and dropped the hilt.

'I might as well stand there and say, "Ho, Fafnir, I am your breakfast!"' he said.

'Give me a day and you will see such a sword as you crave,'

promised Regin. Sigurd sat on his favourite stool by the forge fire and stared into the flames. The red coals seemed full of dragon's breath, and gold, and blood.

Regin worked all night on the new sword, but the result was the same. One blow on the anvil shattered the sword, and Sigurd's hopes. He left the forge without saying a word, and went to dinner in the Hall.

'Why so quiet tonight?' asked Hiordis.

'I have no sword strong enough or sharp enough for any great deed,' said Sigurd. 'Regin is a fine smith but he can only make swords fit for ordinary warriors, not for a great hero as my father was.'

Hiordis smiled at the young man's eagerness. All that seemed so long ago. She went to her chamber and came back with the pieces of Sigmund's sword.

'This is Cleave, your father's sword,' she said, not realising that Sigurd had found the sword as a child. 'Take it to Regin and see if he can mend it for you.'

Sigurd thanked his mother and went out to the forge.

'Mend this for me, your best friend, with all the skill you have. Only with this sword will I set out to kill your dragon.'

When Sigurd came to the forge next, Regin handed him Cleave, the sword of his father Sigmund, mended. Sigurd ran his fingers along the blade, feeling for the joints he knew were there, but it was all as smooth as honey. Suddenly he raised the sword over his head and brought it down on the anvil. Like knife into butter Cleave passed through the iron and into the earth below. Silently, Regin pulled some strands of sheep's wool from a cushion and dropped them into the trough of water that stood next to the divided anvil. Sigurd drew his sword through the water. The floating wool was cut neatly. The two men smiled at each other.

'When do we start?'

So the Norns wove and the pattern came round. The Curse of the Ring pulled Sigurd to Fafnir's cave.

The Slaying of the Dragon

I T was evening. They had travelled for weeks through increasingly desolate country. Forests had thinned and become rough hillside. The ground was uneven and boggy in places so that the horses had to pick their way with care in the failing light. There was no life, except the continual whine of mosquitoes. The high fervour they had set off with weeks ago had been washed out by the driving rain.

'We are very close now,' said Regin suddenly.

Sigurd laughed bitterly. This was not the Great Quest of his dreams. 'Where is the prosperous farm you were driven from?' he asked. 'I

would have been grateful to any dragon that made me leave this place.'

'We have come the other way,' said Regin. 'Over that ridge the land drops sharply down into a fertile valley.'

Sigurd grunted. He was cold, wet, and hungry. He was also beginning to doubt Regin's story. He patted Swift's neck and pulled his cloak more tightly around himself. The heroic deeds that had fired his heart had not dwelt on the discomforts of the journey. His thoughts were interrupted by Regin tugging his sleeve and pointing.

There, in front of them, going straight down the hillside, was a track. In the gloom of evening it looked as if it had been made of cinders from some nearby forge. Sigurd got down from Swift and walked towards it. Just then the full moon came out from behind a cloud and shone, silvering the track. Sigurd thought at once of snail-paths. He stopped at its edge and bent down. It was slimy, and scorched: scorched by Fafnir's poisonous breath, slimed by his oozing body. Sigurd straightened up, feeling sick, and walked back to where Regin was holding the horses.

'You did not tell me it would be like this.'

'Sigurd, I did not know, it has been a long time, he must have grown, and grown worse, from lying on the gold in solitary greed.' Then greed for the gold glowed again in Regin's heart and overcame his loathing and fear. 'But if you are too frightened, Sigurd, then we will return to Ilf's Hall. It will make a story for the winter evenings, I suppose.'

Sigurd had courage enough to face Fafnir, but not enough to face shame.

'You are the expert on this worm,' he said. 'What's your advice? Shall I stand outside and challenge him, or run after him with muffled footsteps?'

Regin smiled. He had brooded for years over his lost share of Andvari's gold. He craved the gold and he wanted revenge on his brother. He had seen the dragon Fafnir and feared him. He had studied

36

all that was known about dragons and knew how to kill one, and what to do with its blood and its heart when it was dead. All through the journey his craving had grown and had swamped completely his love for Sigurd.

'You dig a pit in the middle of the path, get in, cover yourself with branches, and stab once into his heart as he crawls overhead.'

'I dig, do I? What will you be doing?'

'I must take the horses well away. If Fafnir scents them he will eat them. If they smell him they will bolt in terror.'

With you safely in the saddle, thought Sigurd, but what he said was, 'And what shall I dig with?'

Regin smiled again and produced a spade-head and handle from a saddle-bag. He banged a nail in with his hammer, and handed the spade to Sigurd.

'You must dig tonight,' he said, 'or Fafnir may sense us.' And your courage may fail if you see him, he thought. 'The dragon will come out at dawn. I will bring the horses back soon after. Here is a blanket. Use it first to remove the earth.'

Sigurd watched Regin ride away and then he turned and walked grim-faced to the middle of the track that stretched silver in the moonlight. Once he had broken through the crusty surface he found the digging easy in the peaty soil. He dug a hole deep enough to take him, and his sword Cleave, and with room to strike upwards. He dragged the spoil well clear and went down to a blackened copse near the stream to gather wood and leaves to cover the top of his hole.

When Sigurd had dropped in and pulled the branches over himself he had nothing to do but think of the morning, to go over and over in his mind what he had to do. Suddenly he clambered out of his hole and sat on the side, shivering with cold and fear. He had seen his sword pierce the dragon's heart, had seen the dragon's body collapse on the hole, had seen himself desperately clawing his way out while the dragon's blood gushed downwards and drowned him in its red tide.

As he grew calmer he remembered stories of dragons and how if you bathed in their blood no sword or sharp instrument could puncture your skin. So Sigurd picked up his spade and dug a gutter from his hole to drain off the blood so that he would be safe from drowning. Then, as the first light of dawn was just greying the sky, he took off his clothes and waited with calm resolve. He could not see that a dead leaf had stuck in the middle of his back with the sweat of his digging.

The sky had filled with the red light of dawn when Sigurd knew that the dragon was coming. He felt it in the earth around him as Fafnir pulled his weight down to water. He heard the sliding of the scales over the well-rubbed track. He smelt the fumes of poisonous breath. But he could see nothing but the red sky through the lattice of the branches.

Then the pit was filled with the reek of the beast and Sigurd fought for breath. Blackness filled his eyes as the great head covered the hole. Sigurd raised his sword so that it rested lightly on the dragon's underside, like a pointed twig. He could feel the scales grating over Cleave's point one by one. He waited, tensed, for the sudden change, for the feel of bald skin where scales had been rubbed off, where Fafnir had rested his heart on his pile of gold.

Each scale ended in a slight ridge which dragged the sword's point a little before it sprang up under Sigurd's delicate pressure on to the next scale along. Sigurd found he was counting to control his impatience. Then, suddenly, unmistakeably, from one scale's slight drag, no click,

38

no scrape, but a soft resistance. Up he thrust Cleave, pushing with his shoulders and straightening his knees, pushing with his eyes shut as the hot stinking blood began to flood down, pushing until the hilt of his sword struck the skin.

So Sigurd stood with his arms above his head, naked in the red flow cascading down like a waterfall over the rocks of his body. As he stood he heard Fafnir's dying cry, cursing. Then the great body shuddered once, and was still. Sigurd the Dragon-Slayer wearily picked up his spade and dug through the dirt wall of his prison, out into the dirty light of dawn.

He walked down to the stream to wash off Fafnir's blood which was now drying on him. Here Regin found him, and filled him with praise. He made Sigurd tell him every detail of what had happened. Regin's sharp eyes did not miss the leaf on Sigurd's back, but he said nothing about it.

When Sigurd was clean and dressed again Regin said, 'I must now ask a favour, Sigurd. As you know, Fafnir was my brother. So that guilt will not fall on me for my part in his death I must eat his cooked heart. Then this whole sad business will be over and we can collect the gold and return in glory. But you must cut it out, cook it, and offer it to me.'

Regin helped collect wood for a fire but when Sigurd went to cut out Fafnir's heart Regin said, 'I will go and look in Fafnir's cave to see if we can carry the gold on our horses.' So Regin went up the hill, eager to see the gold, and busy with his plans. Sigurd came back with the dragon's heart, sharpened a stick to use as a spit, and put the meat to roast over the fire. After his sleepless night and the tension of the slaying he was drowsy and dozed in the heat.

After some time he jerked awake, looked round anxiously, but saw nothing to alarm him and no sign of Regin. The countryside looked less bleak in the morning sun and already birds were singing in the trees. The fire had died down while he had been asleep. He put out his finger to see if the heart was cooked, burnt the finger on the hot meat, and put it into his mouth to cool it. The taste of the juices ran over his tongue.

'Silly Sigurd,' came a voice, 'sucking his finger like a baby, cooking the dragon's heart for another.'

Sigurd looked up, half-expecting to see Odin disguised as an old

man again, but there was no one in sight. Then another voice came.

'Doesn't he know that he could understand the speech of us birds if he ate some of it?'

Then Sigurd realised what had happened and hastily cut off a corner of Fafnir's heart, blew on it to cool it, and ate it. He left most for his friend, Regin. He could understand all of the birds in the trees now, but what they said was of no interest to him: talk of flies, and territories, and fleas. With their gentle voices in his ears and the warm meat in his stomach he dozed off again.

Sigurd was woken by insistent cries of alarm from the birds: 'A knife! A knife! A knife!' He turned quickly and saw Regin standing above him, knife pointing to where the middle of his back had been. On

his arm, a gold ring shining in the sun; on his face, greed.

Sigurd spoke calmly to his friend. He could not believe what his eyes saw.

'Regin, what is the matter? Look, here is Fafnir's heart ready cooked. Come, eat.'

Regin snarled like a dog with a bone. Then he leapt on Sigurd and tried to stab his back. His blacksmith's muscles strained. As Sigurd jerked his arm to free himself Regin slipped and the knife went into his own flesh. In his dying convulsions the Ring was thrown off his arm and landed by Sigurd, almost as if it had flown there.

Sigurd ignored it and knelt down by Regin. He tried to stop the blood flowing from Regin's chest but could do nothing.

'Forgive me, it is the gold. Beware...' gasped Regin and then he died. Sigurd wept bitterly. Regin had been as a father to him, and then his only true friend. Now, at the moment of their triumph, through some sudden madness it seemed to Sigurd, he had tried to kill him.

Sigurd collected branches, hacked wood from the dead trees, and built a funeral pyre as best he could. He placed Regin's body on it and put his blacksmith's hammer in his hands. He called on Thor to protect him with his greater hammer and set light to the wood. As he stood sadly by the fire he thought of the past years. Had Regin been pretending all this time, since he had first tottered into his forge as a tiny child? Had he really cared nothing for Sigurd, but merely used him for his own revenge?

The birds spoke directly to him. 'Foolish Sigurd! Do not brood over what is past. Travel south. What is there will be worth your journey.'

'Sigurd, has not our advice been good? Do as we say. Go to the hill Hindfell. There is a high Hall ringed about with leaping flames. Seek there for happiness.'

Sigurd turned at last from the desolate hillside where he had killed Fafnir and Regin and walked towards the horses. The glint of gold caught his eye and he bent down and picked up the Ring, Andvaranaut, from where it had fallen. He was about to slip it on his wrist when Swift nuzzled his arm. He patted him, dropped the Ring into his saddle-bag, and rode towards the south. Fafnir's gold could wait. The ring of fire called him.

Brynhild

ON the top of the hill stood a Hall, a Hall a great lord might have built. But no lord could have defended his hall as this one was. Greedy flames made a ring around it; flames that seemed to burn from nothing but whose heat beat Sigurd back. They flickered towards him as if eager to eat him. All else was still, silent.

Sigurd sat on Swift's back and looked at the flames and the Hall. The birds had, as they had said, given good advice until now. Was this a trap? Anything was better than the aching sadness that filled him now that Regin was dead. He patted Swift's neck and set him towards the flames. The horse did not flinch but leapt them easily. It seemed to

45

Sigurd that they died down as he crossed them but when he looked back they were as high as ever.

He left Swift cropping the fresh grass outside the Hall and walked towards the doors. All was quite still. The doors swung open to his hand and he stepped inside. Sunlight streamed past him into the Hall and shone on the golden armour of a figure lying on a table. Sigurd stood and looked. The Hall was well furnished, clean, and empty except for this one motionless figure.

At last Sigurd walked into the Hall and up to the table. The figure was that of a warrior in full gold armour, so heavy, Sigurd thought, that no one could have moved in it. He put his hands to the helmet to try to take it off but it seemed to have no fastenings and would not move. The rest of the armour seemed to be joined invisibly too; there was no way of removing it.

Sigurd walked all round. All was the same. He took Cleave and delicately cut through the gold rings of the chain-mail armour with its point. He lifted the halved helmet from the face of the motionless figure, and dropped it in surprise. This was no warrior, but a beautiful woman whose golden hair now fell to the floor. Still she did not wake. Sigurd cut off the body armour and removed it. Then he saw a long thorn in her wrist. He pulled it out and she immediately opened her eyes.

'You are Sigurd, the bravest of men,' she said.

'I am Sigurd, certainly,' he said. 'Who are you? How do you know my name?'

The woman said nothing, but smiled and led Sigurd to a table in a corner of the Hall that he had not noticed before. There was food and wine, all fresh, all of the best Sigurd had seen.

'Eat and drink, for you are hungry, tired, and sad,' she said.

When Sigurd had finished his meal she led him outside to a seat in the sunshine.

'I am Brynhild. I was a Valkyrie, a daughter of Odin. I am now a mortal woman. I have been waiting for you.'

Sigurd looked at Brynhild in disbelief. The Valkyries were Odin's daughters indeed and were not mortal women. They were fierce and delighted in war. They rode over the battlefields in their golden armour

collecting those Odin wanted for Valhalla. They rode through the thickest of the battle so that blood streamed from them. Their cries filled brave warriors' hearts with terror. Brynhild was clean, quiet, beautiful: a woman to love, not fear.

'I will tell you my story,' she said, 'and then you may believe me. I was once a Valkyrie like the others, rejoicing in blood and mutilation and violent death. One day Odin sent me to kill a young warrior who was fighting an old man. Odin had promised victory to the old man so I had to slaughter a handsome youth. I could not do it this time. The young man still had his life to lead. I shattered the old man's sword. He had had his day.' Brynhild did not tell Sigurd that the old man was his own father, Sigmund, and that the handsome young man was Lyngvi, whom he had sworn to kill. Nor did she tell him that the sword she had shattered was Cleave, the sword in his own hands.

'What did Odin say?'

Brynhild did not answer at first. Odin's rage had been terrible. Asgard had shaken and she had cowered from him.

'He made me a mortal,' she said eventually.

'That is a dreadful punishment,' said Sigurd, though he could not begin to realise how dreadful. 'But why the Hall, the ring of fire?'

Again Brynhild was lost in memory before she answered. Her awful punishment showed how much Odin had loved Sigmund. He must care, too, for this young man.

'He said I was to wait for a man who deserved me. I must marry any man who was able to jump the flames. Till he came I was to sleep out of time. He said Sigurd, Dragon-Slayer, should be that man.'

Sigurd looked at her, and loved filled his heart. He got up, went over to Swift, and took the Ring from his saddle-bag.

'This is a token of my love,' he said, and placed it over her wrist. And so Andvari's curse fell on Brynhild at the moment of happiness. Odin had hoped to give Sigurd happiness with Brynhild to make up for the death of his father. But even Odin's plans were part of the weaving of the Norns, and nothing fell out as he wanted.

Sigurd stayed with Brynhild in her Hall and they lived as husband and wife with great contentment. Sigurd told Brynhild his whole story. It was, perhaps, the Ring that reminded him at last of his vow to avenge his father so that he became restless.

'I must go and find Lyngvi,' he said. 'But I will return to you at once and then we will collect Fafnir's gold and return to Ilf's court to my mother.'

Brynhild looked at him sadly, full of foreboding. 'Place the thorn of sleep back in my wrist, Sigurd, and then I can wait patiently.'

She lay on the table and Sigurd pricked her with the thorn and she was at once fast asleep. He kissed her, and left the Hall. As Swift jumped the ring of fire the flames again seemed to die down, but as he looked back they flickered as hungrily as ever. Sigurd set out to avenge his father.

Gudrun

SIGURD reined-in Swift and looked down on the settlement below. He had travelled for several days from Brynhild's Hall but this journey had been different. The sun had been shining and his heart was filled with love. He had slain the dragon and won fame, gold, and lady.

The lands he had come to were ruled by the widow-queen, Grimhild. She was clever enough to appear pleasant and sympathetic. She was beautiful, in a dark, gloomy way, and captivated men. The passions of her heart were her three sons, and witchcraft. Her eldest son, Gunnar, was her especial favourite. Gunnar was an honest man but in his mother's spell. The two younger sons were Hogni and Gotthorn. They had a sister, Gudrun, a gentle girl with none of her mother's evil in her. It was to Grimhild's snare that the Norns brought Sigurd.

Travellers were always welcome because they brought news, and new faces. The arrival of the man who had just killed a dragon was a story to tell one's grandchildren. Sigurd was feted as he rode through the streets and Grimhild herself came out to meet him. She showed him every honour and pressed him to stay there for a few days.

'I must not stop for more than one night,' he replied. 'I go to avenge my father.'

That night, at dinner in the Hall, Sigurd's tongue ran away with him and he told of his story more than was wise. He told of the slaying of Fafnir and made it sound like man against monster out on the dawn field. He did not explain that he had cowered in a hole and ambushed the dragon. And somehow Regin disappeared from the story. Then he lowered his voice and told to Queen Grimhild alone of the winning of Brynhild, of her beauty and grace.

'But tell no one of this,' he said. 'My marriage is a secret until I can bring her to my mother's Hall.'

Grimhild hated the easy self-confidence of this puppy. Why should he have what her deserving children lacked? She whispered instructions to her servant-woman. Sigurd's next cup of wine tasted especially sweet. He turned to thank Grimhild for it. She leant towards him and spoke very softly:

'You will forget Brynhild. Forget you have seen her. Forget you have married her. Forget you love her. You came straight here after killing Fafnir.' Then she raised her voice. 'Gudrun, come here and entertain our hero with your singing.'

So Gudrun sat at Sigurd's feet and sang songs of love to him, and looked lovingly up at him from under her dark hair. And Sigurd, whose heart knew he was in love, thought he was in love with her. She was a girl whom it was easy to love.

Sigurd woke next day, in love with Gudrun, and was married.

'Why should we wait,' said Queen Grimhild, 'when you are obviously fated for each other?'

Gudrun was overwhelmed by love. If Sigurd felt an occasional sadness he believed it was Regin's death that caused it. As he had forgotten Brynhild he forgot too his quest to avenge his father. But the gold he did not forget. Grimhild sent him with her sons to fetch it.

The obvious happiness that shone out of Gudrun like sunlight off gold seemed to irritate the Queen. She wanted Gunnar to share his sister's good fortune. So it was not many weeks before she started inciting Gunnar to seek Brynhild for his wife.

'Take Sigurd with you,' she said. 'It will be good for him to live rough in the open air. He's getting soft.'

Sigurd laughed and agreed willingly enough. He loved Gudrun but found the atmosphere of Grimhild's court uneasy. He kissed his wife goodbye and the two men set off on a fine autumn morning. They had an easy ride through the yellowing woods and over the hillsides covered with bilberries. They travelled from village to village, and then slept out in the open until, fit and cheerful, they came in sight of Brynhild's Hall.

Both men reined-in their horses. Both had heard from Grimhild of the ring of fire; neither had any idea of its fierce hunger all but hiding the Hall beyond.

'And Brynhild is beyond that barrier of flames?' asked Gunnar.

'So I am told,' said Sigurd. 'How will you get through?'

'Mother said I should jump over the fire.'

Gunnar pointed his horse at the Hall and kicked him with his spurs but the terrified beast reared and screamed. Gunnar took off his cloak and tied it over the horse's head so that it could not see but it felt the

heat of the fire and would not jump. However much Gunnar spurred it, hit it or shouted, the horse would not go near. Finally, with the animal shaking and foaming at the mouth, with blood running down its flanks, Gunnar gave up.

'Lend me Swift,' he said.

Sigurd made him promise to use no whip or spur before he would agree. Then Gunnar leapt on Swift's back and urged him forwards. He would not move one step. Sigurd smiled.

'No one but me has ever sat on his back before. I do not think he will obey you.'

Gunnar cursed. Then he recovered his good humour as he thought of a solution.

'Perhaps you can jump Swift over the flames and carry Brynhild out for me.' As Sigurd mounted again, he said, 'Wait! My mother told me that Brynhild was bound to marry the first man who braved the fire. She must believe that you are me.'

'She will never do that,' said Sigurd, 'we are quite different. No one could mistake us.'

'My mother has strange powers. She has taught me a few tricks of illusion. I can make you look exactly like me.'

Gunnar muttered under his breath and snapped his fingers. There was a second Gunnar, alike in every way, sitting on a horse identical to Gunnar's. Gunnar smiled at his new twin.

'I will wait in that copse down by the stream. Ride down, leave Brynhild by the stream and walk into the trees until you are out of sight. I will change you back and take her from you.'

Sigurd agreed to all this with some misgivings. He was an honourable man and disliked deceit but events had developed a momentum of their own. Besides, Gunnar would have braved the fire for Brynhild; it was his horse that was unwilling. He set Swift towards the fire and the horse jumped easily. It seemed to Sigurd that the flames died down as he crossed them but when he looked back they were as high as ever.

He left Swift cropping the fresh grass outside the Hall and walked towards the doors. All was quiet. The doors swung open to his hand

and he stepped inside. Sunlight streamed past him into the Hall and shone on the golden hair of the woman lying on the table.

Sigurd walked into the Hall and up to the table. He wondered at her beauty and stillness. Then he saw a long thorn in her wrist. He pulled it out and immediately she opened her eyes.

'You are not Sigurd,' she said.

Sigurd looked at her in surprise. 'I am Gunnar,' he said, 'eldest son of Queen Grimhild. I know Sigurd well; he is married to my sister.'

At these words Brynhild's heart died within her.

'Very well. I am to marry the man brave enough to cross the ring of fire. I will marry you if you wish it.'

As Brynhild bowed her head and clasped her hands together she felt the Ring on her wrist and an ache of longing for Sigurd filled her. She wished to delay leaving as long as possible, partly in the hope that Sigurd would ride up at the last moment, partly in the dread of meeting him at Grimhild's court.

'It is getting late. Let us sleep here tonight and ride out in the morning.'

Grim-faced, she led Sigurd to a table in the corner of the Hall that he had not noticed before. There was food and wine, all fresh, all of the best Sigurd had seen.

'Eat and drink, Gunnar,' she said.

When Sigurd had finished his meal—she was too heart-broken to eat—she led him to her bed chamber. Sigurd drew his sword and laid it down in the middle of the bed.

'I will marry you at court,' he said, promising for Gunnar. He was an honourable man and he loved Gudrun. And so they slept that night—side by side, lifetimes apart.

In the morning Sigurd noticed the Ring on Brynhild's wrist.

'Give me that ring as a token of our betrothal,' he said. He planned to give it to Gunnar in the wood.

'No!' said Brynhild. 'I cannot.'

'It must be a love-token from some other man,' said Sigurd. 'That is all the more reason why you should now give it to me. The past is past.'

Brynhild gave him the Ring in despair. Sigurd's love for her was past indeed and so hers must be too.

'Here, Gunnar, my lord,' she said. 'May it seal our happiness.'

Sigurd slipped the Ring on his wrist, picked up his sword, and led Brynhild to Swift. He placed her on his back and got up behind. As they trotted towards the ring of fire the flames died down, and were gone. The green grass stretched down the hillside. Sigurd looked behind him. Brynhild's Hall was thinning until it seemed to festoon the hill-top like cobwebs. A puff of wind – it was gone.

They rode down the hill in the morning mist. Neither could see what lay ahead. When they reached the copse by the stream Sigurd said:

'We will rest here a little while. Excuse me while I go into the wood.'

Brynhild did not answer, but sat staring blankly at the water. Sigurd led Swift into the trees. Gunnar burst through the bushes towards him.

'What happened? Why have you been so long? What have you done?'

Sigurd spoke to him calmly, telling him in every detail what had happened. For some reason he could not explain to himself, he did not mention the Ring but kept it hidden under his sleeve. Satisfied, Gunnar spoke the words that undid the spell of illusion and Sigurd and Swift were themselves again.

'I will go back by a different way,' Sigurd said. 'We will meet later as if we had been separated for days.'

And so Sigurd rode off to Gudrun and Gunnar came out from the trees and spoke kindly to Brynhild, for he loved her at first sight. They, too, returned to Queen Grimhild's court.

'Let Confusion Ring him Round'

As the Norns bent over their weaving Sigurd returned to Queen Grimhild's Hall. Gudrun met him and asked him what had happened. He told her that all had gone as planned; Gunnar had leapt the ring of flames and won Brynhild.

'What is she like?'

'Beautiful, but cold. Hair like gold. Almost silent.'

As Sigurd told her the story he raised his arm to describe how Gunnar's horse had jumped. His sleeve fell back and showed the Ring.

'What is that Ring? Show me!'

Sigurd passed it to Gudrun. She turned it in her hands, looking at the coiling serpents. Then she burst into tears.

'Some woman has given you this.'

Sigurd was distressed by her grief and her suspicion. He swore her to secrecy and then told her the truth about the winning of Brynhild.

'But why did you not give the Ring to Gunnar in the wood?'

'I do not know. I must have forgotten,' he said.

'It is too late now to give it to Gunnar and you can never wear it in

case Brynhild saw it and guessed the truth. I will put it into my jewel-box.'

And so Gudrun placed the Ring in her box as you might sow a rare seed that will one day produce strange flowers.

That evening Brynhild came to Queen Grimhild's Hall for the first time. All marvelled at her beauty, but marvelled more at the heart of stone she seemed to have. She was cold, like an ice-maiden: polite, correct, unsmiling. Sigurd went up to her with easy warmth for he knew she could not recognise him.

'Welcome, sister,' he said.

Whatever hope lingered in Brynhild's heart died at these words. Sigurd seemed to have forgotten her completely. He showed no embarrassment or shame. He took pride in introducing his wife to her. Brynhild was too proud to say anything, except 'Thank you.' She turned from him and looked into the fire.

Around her, Grimhild's Hall was full of noise and movement. No one seemed quiet or still. Jokes were made, tricks were played. They were all, perhaps, a little unkind but drink blurred the barbs. Brynhild alone sat aloof, still.

'Cold indeed,' said Gudrun to her husband.

Early next morning Sigurd and his wife's brothers went riding. As Gotthorn, the youngest, led his horse out it seemed to limp.

'Curse the Norns!' he shouted. 'I shall miss my ride today.'

The others shouted cheerfully back at him and rode on. They came to a hilltop overlooking steep valleys that ran down to the distant sea. They turned and smiled at each other, feeling secure in their friendship and fully alive in the crisp morning air.

'I owe you everything,' Gunnar said to Sigurd. 'How can I ever repay you?'

'I could do no less,' Sigurd replied, 'for the brother of my wife, for my friend.'

'Let us swear oaths of brotherhood to each other now, now before I marry Brynhild,' Gunnar said.

'I too will swear,' said Hogni, 'for our home has changed since you came. Gotthorn is too young for such serious oaths. The Norns obviously meant his horse to go lame so that he should not feel left out.'

'I will swear willingly,' said Sigurd. He drew Cleave from its scabbard and the three men placed their hands on it and promised to be faithful until death. The early morning sun flushed red behind them.

Next day Gunnar and Brynhild were married. At the wedding feast Queen Grimhild looked around the table. On her right hand was Gunnar, happy in the beauty of his wife. On her left was Brynhild, icy. Opposite, Gudrun and Sigurd, content with each other. Her younger sons were laughing together at a servant they had tripped up. All this was of her doing: the family in a ring around her. A spiteful desire to have her power known filled her. She leant over the table towards Sigurd. She put her hand on his wrist where the Ring had once rested.

'Remember!' she said.

Sigurd looked across the table at Brynhild. He went white, cried

out, and stumbled from the Hall. Gudrun got up to follow him but her mother said:

'It will be best to leave him. I think he is not used to much drink.'

Gudrun sat down slowly. She did not think Sigurd was drunk but she was not used to disobeying her mother.

Sigurd walked away from the settlement into the woods. He cried aloud, wept, and cursed. He remembered everything and understood everything. His passion for Brynhild once more filled his heart while despair filled his mind. What could he do? What was Brynhild thinking? No wonder she had said 'You are not Sigurd!' He could saddle horses and ride off with Brynhild away from this witches' den. He could ride with her back to his mother's court. He could go anywhere—he had all Fafnir's gold.

Sigurd strode back to Grimhild's Hall and looked through an open doorway. He looked with longing at Brynhild. No wonder she was cold, silent. He could turn that misery to fierce joy. Then he looked at Gudrun. His love for Gudrun had been washed away in the flood of his returning memory. He saw her, from the darkness outside, casting worried glances at the doorway and at Queen Grimhild. He did not love

61

Gudrun, but he pitied her with all his heart. Her mother had tricked her as much as she had tricked him. Gudrun had done no wrong. How could he destroy her? And how could he hurt Gunnar, to whom he had sworn eternal brotherhood that very morning?

As Sigurd stood there he thought of arriving at his mother's Hall with Gunnar and his men in fast pursuit behind them. He thought of the battles and feuds that would involve both families. He put his hand down to touch the Ring as he thought of Brynhild and her love but it was not on his wrist. Sigurd walked back into the Hall and sat down next to Gudrun. He smiled at her and went on with the meal.

Months passed. Unhappiness grew. Sigurd did his best to act as if nothing had changed but Gudrun could feel that her husband's love had gone from her. Gunnar found his wife polite and obedient but cold and distant. Sigurd and Brynhild were locked in their secret misery. They did not speak to each other, except politely, in company. He had not told Brynhild of the trick that had been played on him, or of the trick that had been played on her. Gudrun tried to like Brynhild for her brother's sake, but to her Brynhild could hardly hide her hatred. So unhappiness spread like a ring of ripples from the spell dropped by Queen Grimhild into Sigurd's mind.

One hot, sultry day Brynhild walked down to the stream to bathe herself. She found Gudrun there before her. Brynhild's pride and unhappiness would not let her smile and bathe with Gudrun, but the water looked cool in the heat. She walked upstream a little and waded into the water. Black clouds of mud streamed down towards Gudrun.

'Come and bathe here,' said Gudrun. 'The bottom is fine gravel.'

Brynhild looked at her smiling face. There Gudrun stood, washing that body that Sigurd loved, smiling. How Brynhild hated her!

'I will not wash in water that has touched your flesh,' she said.

Gudrun's patience broke as she thought of the Ring in her jewel-box. 'What is so superior about you? Why will you never talk to me?'

Brynhild laughed scornfully. 'Talk to you! What could I talk to you about? I was a Valkyrie, a daughter of Odin. I have flown over battlefields collecting the noblest of warriors at my father's command, taking them to Valhalla. Am I now to talk to you of fine gravel, and washing?'

'My husband is the noblest warrior living, for he killed the dragon Fafnir.'

'That is nothing. My husband leapt through a ring of fire for me. No one would do that for you.'

63

Gudrun laughed. 'Your husband did nothing. He tried but failed. Sigurd had to do it for him, in his likeness.'

'That is a childish lie,' said Brynhild. 'You are as spiteful as the rest of your family.'

'If you do not believe me then ask Gunnar where he keeps the Ring you gave him.'

Brynhild started. Why had she forgotten the Ring? She had not thought of it once since she had left the Hall on that unhappy morning.

'I expect Gunnar has it safe,' she said.

'Yes, indeed,' laughed Gudrun, 'safe in my jewel-box. Sigurd put it there. Sigurd took it off his own wrist. Sigurd gave it to me.'

Brynhild waded through the stream and grasped Gudrun's arm. 'Show me, now!'

Silently they dressed and walked back through the birch wood to Gudrun's chamber. There Gudrun opened her jewel-box and showed Brynhild the Ring, curled up like a contented cat.

Brynhild walked to her own chamber and threw herself on her bed. She would not speak, or eat, or drink. When Gunnar came near she threw things at him until he left her. Gunnar went to find Sigurd.

'Brynhild is in a rage and will not speak to me. Would you, my brother, talk to her for me and make peace between us? I do not even know what I have done wrong.'

Sigurd walked into Brynhild's chamber and stood looking at her, tears sliding down his cheeks. Gudrun had told him what she had said and he could guess Brynhild's bitterness. Quietly, he told her the whole story of his bewitching and he told her of his love for her that burned as fiercely as ever, of the anguish of his own heart.

'Then let us leave together, now,' she begged him, clinging to him.

'I could never leave Gudrun,' he said, and gently laid her back on the bed. 'She has done nothing wrong. Her mother bewitched us. Gudrun is gentle and honourable. I cannot hurt her. Besides, her brothers would not rest until she was avenged.'

'You cannot love me if you can speak like that! I, a Valkyrie, offer you my heart and body and you weigh it up so reasonably! What is Gudrun, that milksop, that mewling child, to you? When I am here?' Brynhild tore at her hair and scratched at her face. Sigurd tried to

restrain her, and begged her to be calm. 'How can I be calm? How dare you speak to me in that way—as if I was some, some housewife!'

Bitter anger seized Brynhild and she would not speak to Sigurd again. When her husband returned she said to him:

'You are a fool. You should never have invited Sigurd to my bedchamber. When he came to me in my Hall pretending to be you— and how could you believe I would be taken in—he forced me to sleep with him that night when we were together inside the ring of fire. And just now, when you invited him into our marriage room he forced me on to our bed and only left when I screamed. He will not rest until he has dishonoured you again. He must be killed.'

Gunnar looked at Brynhild. She stood there, pale, beautiful. How could he not believe her? But how could he believe that Sigurd would trick him so?

'You must have mistaken his natural kindness,' he said at last. 'Sigurd is a loyal friend and would not hurt me.'

'*You*—hurt *you?*' screamed Brynhild. 'It is I that he has hurt, has shamed, has wronged!'

Gunnar stood there shaking his head. He was confused and did not know what to think. Then Brynhild stopped shouting and very coldly and calmly described Sigurd's naked body in such detail that Gunnar had to believe her.

'He will die,' he said, and left Brynhild and went to find his brothers. He told them what Brynhild had said.

'I can hardly believe this of Sigurd,' Gunnar said. 'But I must, and Sigurd must die. But I cannot kill him because I have sworn an oath of brotherhood with him.'

'And I,' said Hogni, the middle brother. 'You, Gotthorn, must kill him, now.'

The three brothers went in search of Sigurd and saw him lying on the bank of the stream. He was face down, his tears watering the flowers. The two older brothers waited among the trees while Gotthorn crept up and stabbed Sigurd between the shoulder blades. He did not know that Sigurd had bathed in Fafnir's blood but fate directed his dagger to the leaf's shadow. Sigurd, twisting in his dying agony, picked up Cleave and hurled it with his remaining strength at Gotthorn. The sword sliced through Gotthorn so that his body fell different ways. So Sigurd died.

Then a great funeral pyre was built and Sigurd's body was placed on it, his sword Cleave in his hand. Brynhild came down and looked in Sigurd's face. All anger drained from her and she knew only the desperation of love.

'Sigurd!' she cried out. 'I will come with you to the land of the dead. I would rather be in Hel with you than ride the storm winds with my sisters.'

She seized Cleave and thrust it into her heart, and fell dead on the pyre. So Sigurd and Brynhild lay side by side again, the sword between them. This time no one could part them. There lay together Sigurd the Dragon-Slayer and Brynhild the Valkyrie. The Norns had woven their fates into their tapestry and they had been powerless against the Curse of the Ring. With their deaths the Ring itself passed from the hands of great heroes into those of greedy men.

So the pyre was lit and a ring of flames surrounded Sigurd and Brynhild. When the fire died down their ashes blew away in the wind, and were gone. Gudrun's eyes followed them out of sight.

'Fill her Heart with Emptiness.'

WHEN her women had come to tell Gudrun of Sigurd's death she had been so struck with grief that she could not cry out or weep. Two women of the Queen's household had come to comfort her. Each had told Gudrun of the sorrows of their own lives. They had spoken of deaths in battle and deaths at sea, deaths of parents, husbands, children. They had spoken of deaths, of mutilations, madness. They had said that time would help. But Gudrun could not weep.

Then her servant woman had led her to Sigurd's body and uncovered it.

'Look at your lord's body, and kiss him,' she said.

Gudrun had looked at Sigurd. She had seen his hair clotted with blood and his bright eyes closed. Then she fell on him and her tears washed his face and eased the breaking of her heart.

Gudrun had picked up Cleave and said, 'Brynhild may accompany him to the land of the dead while I am left alone with the living but I will have his sword, my Sigurd's sword.'

Queen Grimhild's Hall was not a happy place after the deaths of Sigurd and Brynhild. Gunnar had lost his wife, Gudrun her husband, Grimhild her son. The Queen and Gunnar blamed Sigurd for their loss and so Gudrun became hateful to them. And Gudrun had gold, all Fafnir's hoard, but she had grief enough to cover its glow.

The Norns continued their weaving. The pattern was nearly complete; it had nearly come full circle.

So time passed. Gunnar became King. Grimhild died, though whether of old age, bitterness, or poison no one knew, or cared much. And still Gudrun wandered the rooms like a ghost. Her own Hall became filled with cobwebs. She would let the servants touch nothing. The spiders seemed to weave in mockery of the Norns, and their webs stretched grey, shapeless, meaningless, all around. Gudrun felt at peace in this desolate room, the more so when the cobwebs covered the gold because it had become hateful to her.

News of Fafnir's gold and Sigurd's death came to a nearby king,

Atli. He sent his messenger to ask for Gudrun to be his wife. Gunnar led the messenger to Gudrun's Hall. Through the open door they saw her sitting, grey amidst the festooning webs, all colour gone.

'Here is a messenger from King Atli. He would have you for his wife. What answer shall I give?'

Gudrun shrugged. She knew Atli and disliked him. He was coarse and crude, his people poor. But she could feel nothing for her brothers now and memories of Sigurd filled the Hall.

'If he wishes,' she said.

The messenger departed and Gudrun was got ready. Gunnar would not let her take Fafnir's gold with her because it was entwining itself round his heart. He spoke to wound her so that she would not ask again.

'I will keep it here,' he said. 'Since Sigurd married Brynhild first it should really have been hers, and so mine.'

Again, Gudrun did not care, but she slipped the Ring on her wrist and hid it under her sleeve so that Gunnar should not know she had it. As she put it on she felt hatred blossom in her heart and she would not speak to her brothers. She took with her Sigurd's sword, Cleave, and her memories.

When she arrived at King Atli's Hall and he discovered that the gold had not come with her he was furious and raged at her and struck her. Then he made her sit and write to her brothers and invite them to visit her. If they came, they would surely bring the gold with them. They would not want it out of their sight.

'Write, so that your brothers will be sure to come,' he said. 'And I will read your letter before it is taken over the sea to them.'

Gudrun wrote the letter that Atli expected her to write. As she rested her hand on the table the weight of the Ring on her wrist gave her an idea.

'Brother,' she wrote, 'do this thing and come to see me. As truly as I loved Brynhild do I ask you to come.' Gunnar knows how I hate Brynhild, she thought, he will guess that I have been forced to write this letter and will stay away.

'Have you finished that letter?' Atli asked her. Then he saw the Ring on her wrist and pulled it roughly from her.

'This at least I will have now.'

And so the Ring, with its twisting serpents, took another captive. As it passed from Gudrun her heart lightened and she began to understand its power. She was the daughter of a witch and had brooded long on all that Sigurd had told her of what he had heard from Regin and of what he himself had done. Then she saw how the Ring seemed to work on Atli, heightening all that was evil in him, suppressing all that was good. So she came to guess that Andvari had placed some curse upon the Ring when it was taken.

When Gunnar received his sister's letter, he wept. 'Gudrun always loved Brynhild dearly, until their final misunderstanding,' he said. 'She has now forgiven her and wishes to be reconciled to me. I must go to her at once.'

'I will come with you,' said Hogni. 'I cannot bear this place now.'

Gunnar would not take the gold with him as he did not trust Atli, but he would not leave it at home because he had grown miserly and did not trust anyone there either. He called his brother.

'Help me with these sacks. We will hide Fafnir's gold in the river. Only you and I will know where it is. If anything happens to either of us, the other will be able to retrieve it. It will be safe until we come back.'

They found a small cave under a waterfall where they used to swim as children. Here they left the sacks amid the mouldy straw and old bones that littered the place.

'This must have been some animal's lair,' said Hogni.

'Nothing has been here for years,' said Gunnar. 'All this is stale and decayed.'

The brothers did not realise that they had hidden the gold in Andvari's cave. The Norns had completed this part of the pattern and returned the treasure to its starting point. Here it would rest until Andvari on his desperate wanderings would find it again and remove it to a safer place.

When the brothers arrived at Atli's Hall they looked around with disgust.

'This is some peasant's mud hut,' said Hogni.

Gunnar looked at the earth floor, the rough tables, the pigs and hens running about through the room. Pity for his sister began to grow in his heart.

King Atli greeted them eagerly and helped them with their baggage himself.

'Is this all you have brought?' he asked.

'It is enough for a summer's visit,' they replied.

Gunnar could not understand why Gudrun looked so shocked when she saw them, why she hardly spoke to them. Atli never left them alone for a moment so he could not speak to her of what was in his heart. Atli wore the Ring on his wrist, its bright gold seeming out of place in this squalid place.

Atli controlled his disappointment until night. When all were asleep he had the brothers taken and bound and placed in separate cells. In the morning he came to Gunnar.

'Tell me where my wife's gold is, and you can go free.'

'Your wife has no gold. It was my wife's, Brynhild's.'

Gunnar would say no more than this. Atli sent Gudrun to see her brother, to persuade him to save his life by telling Atli where the gold was. She wept when she saw him, and kissed him. She had brooded long on the past and saw that Gunnar had been a victim of the Ring, as she had been too. She remembered his kindnesses to her as a child in their unhappy home. He was all she had left to love.

'I forgive you the wrong I was done,' she said. 'You were under our mother's enchantments. Do not trust my husband. If you tell him

74

where the gold is he will surely kill you to stop you trying to get it back.'

Gunnar saw that what Gudrun said was true. They talked sadly together and then said goodbye to each other. When King Atli next came, Gunnar said:

'My sister has persuaded me. I cannot see her live here in such poverty when I have all Fafnir's gold. I would tell you but my brother and I took an oath never to reveal where we had hidden the gold. I can never tell you while he lives.'

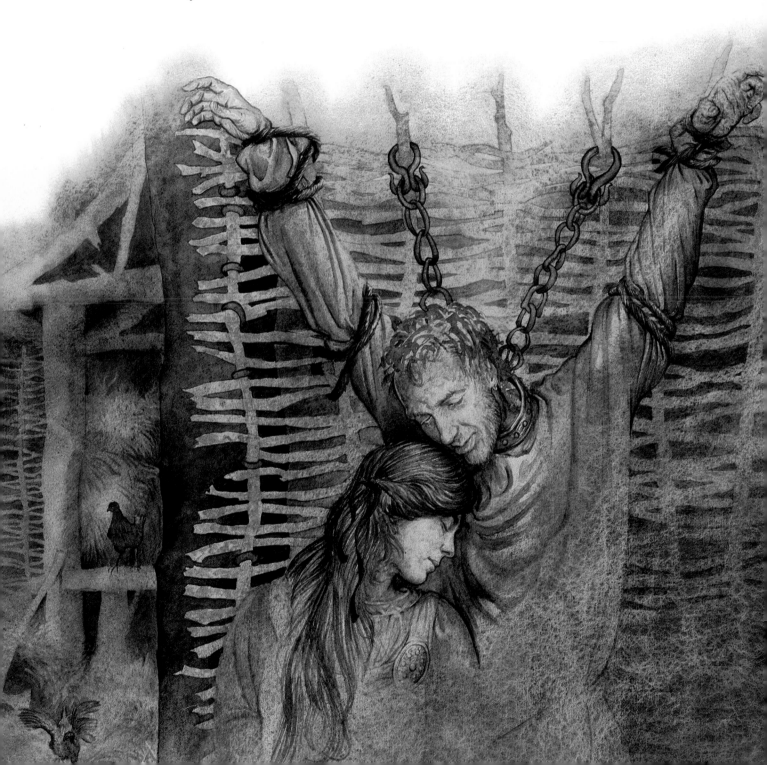

Atli at once ordered that Hogni should be killed and that his head should be cut off. He had it brought in a basket and shown to Gunnar.

'Now that your brother is dead no one will know that you have broken your oath. Tell me where the gold is.'

Gunnar laughed. 'My brother might have told you under torture. Now he has died quickly. He can tell you nothing and you can do him no more harm. I will never tell you. The gold came from a dragon and you are just a worm in a dung-hill.'

Then Atli saw how Gunnar had tricked him. He shouted out with such rage that the cups on the table rattled and the geese in the yard gobbled in fright. He had Gunnar thrown into his snake-pit. There Gunnar lay, bruised, thirsty, looking up at the ring of blue sky above while green and gold serpents twisted around him. He felt at peace and

ready for death. He moved his hand and a snake twisted in a ring around his wrist and bit him. The venom spread through his body and he was dead.

When Gudrun heard that her two brothers were dead she took Sigurd's sword and crept quietly to Atli's chamber. There lay her husband asleep. She closed her eyes, raised Cleave, and brought it down with all her strength. The sharp sword went through his body and sliced off his hand at the wrist. The Ring rolled over the floor and came to rest at her feet.

Gudrun smiled at it. She tied it on Sigurd's sword with a ribbon from her hair. Then she went into the Hall and took a smouldering log from the fire-place. She placed it under Atli's bed.

'Warm yourself, my lord,' she said. 'You will be cold enough in the land of Hel.'

Then she walked out of Atli's Hall, out of the settlement, and down on to the beach. She bent down and washed her hands clean of his blood in the salt water. She stood looking back at his Hall until she saw a ring of flames spring up, burning the bodies of the King and her two brothers. Only then did tears run down her face and fall into the sea.

Slowly Gudrun untied her girdle. It had been woven like the

weaving of the Norns with strange patterns and twisting lines. She picked up Sigurd's sword, the sword that Odin gave to Sigmund, the sword Brynhild broke at his death, the sword Regin mended, and she tied it over her heart. She took the Ring and placed it on her wrist.

Gudrun walked out into the welcoming sea, the waves licking hungrily at her. Then she swam away from the land until tiredness and the weight of the sword pulled her slowly under the water.

THE Ring gleamed. Its gold circle seemed to smile as it lay under the water. The current lifted it slightly, and then dropped it. It seemed to be waiting, coiling round and round like the great serpent of Middle Earth that swallows its own tail. As it shifted in the water it seemed to wink its one eye, as if it knew...